Praise for *Desert Cabal*

"*Desert Cabal* is a grief-song to the American desc̲ scolding, a tumult, a praye̲ Amy Irvine implores us t̲ solidarity, to recognize our ̲ other and in the places we love, so that we might come together to save them. In this time of all out war being waged on America's public lands, I'm glad she's on my side."

—**Pam Houston, author of** *Contents May Have Shifted*

"Amy Irvine is Ed Abbey's underworld, her roots reaching into the dark, hidden water. In a powerful, dreamlike series of essays, she lays *Desert Solitaire* bare, looking back at the man who wrote the book and the desert left behind. This stream of consciousness, this conversation, this broadside, is an alternate version of Abbey's country. It is another voice in the wilderness."

—**Craig Childs, author of** *Atlas of a Lost World*

"If you've ever talked back to the canonical tomes of the environmental movement, this is a book for you. Here are the women, the people, the children, and the intimate dangers those old books so frequently erased. Here is a new and necessary ethic that might help us more openly love the land and the many living beings who share it. I found myself nodding—*Yes! Yes! Thank you!*—on nearly every page of *Desert Cabal*."

—**Camille T. Dungy, author of** *Guidebook to Relative Strangers* **and editor of** *Black Nature*

"Ed Abbey's rise to sainthood has been a bit awkward: here is an earth hero who guzzles gas in search of his personal Eden, a champion of the underdog who snubs

Mexicans and Natives, an anarchist rabble-rouser who utters not a peep about his perch atop the patriarchy. Finally someone—and it could be no better iconoclast than Amy Irvine—wrassles him off the pedestal back down to the red dirt where he belongs. Half riot and half tribute, this is a roadmap through a crisis that neither Abbey nor any of us imagined."

—Mark Sundeen, author of *The Man Who Quit Money*
and *The Unsettlers*

"Amy Irvine lays bare the mostly bleached bones of *Desert Solitaire* fifty years hence. Amy shows an uncanny ability to scrape the joints clean and dig deep into the marrow to find truth. *Desert Cabal* will make you squirm, yet reminds us that Edward Abbey was only human, that our human psyche continues to evolve as does our understanding of life and nature."

—Andy Nettell, Back of Beyond Books

"For those of us who wanted to be Bonnie Abzug, Amy Irvine is a kindred spirit. And she's right; times have changed, Mr. Abbey; we're negotiating tricky territory in the world of environmental rights, especially in the West. Who's right? Who's left? What will remain when the dust settles? *Desert Cabal* is brutally honest, which is just exactly what we need right now."

—Anne Holman, The King's English Bookshop

"If there wasn't a woman in Ed Abbey's trailer in Arches back in the 1950s, there is one now. And she has a room and a voice of her own."

—Ken Sanders, Ken Sanders Rare Books

Desert Cabal
A New Season in the Wilderness

Desert Cabal
A New Season in the Wilderness

AMY IRVINE

 TORREY
HOUSE
PRESS

SALT LAKE CITY
TORREY

 Back of
Beyond
Books

MOAB

First Torrey House Press and Back of Beyond Books Edition,
November 2018

Copyright © 2018 by Amy Irvine

Published by

Torrey House Press
Salt Lake City, Utah
www.torreyhouse.org

Back of Beyond Books
Moab, Utah
www.backofbeyondbooks.com

International Standard Book Number: 978-1-937226-97-8
E-book ISBN: 978-1-937226-96-1
Library of Congress Control Number: 2018948873

Cover art *Red Swell* by Amy O. Woodbury
Cover design by Kathleen Metcalf
Interior design by Rachel Davis
Distributed to the trade by Consortium Book Sales and
Distribution

"The Glass Essay" by Anne Carson, from GLASS, IRONY,
AND GOD, copyright ©1995 by Anne Carson. Reprinted
by permission of New Directions Publishing Corp.

For Devin
All that was lost, now found

CONTENTS

FOREWORD

Nearly two decades ago, I moved to the edge of one of the most rugged and remote landscapes in the American West: Boulder, Utah, bordered by the newly designated Grand Staircase-Escalante National Monument. I had been a Grand Canyon river cook for ten years before this, and had learned firsthand the transformative power of time spent in a protected wild landscape combined with a lovingly prepared meal. I had also been an advocate for public lands all of my adult life, largely informed by my obsession with the writings of Edward Abbey. So when the opportunity arose to open a restaurant in southern Utah's redrock country, I seized it joyfully, and I and a friend—another woman—started a business in a town so tiny and remote that it was the last in the country to receive its mail by mule.

Our concept was simple: we wanted to be a warm hearth for the kind of traveler who was seeking an authentic, heartfelt wilderness experience;

we would offer a place to gather before and after the journey, a welcoming room in which to be received and fed. We were proud to be women business owners in old-fashioned southern Utah, and proud of our work: we were delighted to bring everyone to the table. Deeply committed to our new community and fostering ideas of sustain-ability, we started a farm and hired locally, paying everyone a living wage. But more than anything, we wanted to help people fall in love with this high mountain desert through the intimate act of feeding them food literally *of this place*. Think of it as culinary activism: help guests develop a devotion to the land, and they will be moved to speak and act on its behalf.

During my camp cook days, deep in the Grand Canyon, on the banks of the Colorado River, I had held the hands of visitors who were shaken to the core by the profundity of absolute quiet. I had wiped their tears as they sobbed over the almost unbearable magnitude of beauty. I often asked them to imagine what the state of the place would be today, had it not been protected more than a hundred years ago.

I ask this again, this horrid imagining—only now I ask it of everyone I encounter, and I ask on behalf of the wild, rugged redrock country where I live. What will the state of *this* place be, in fifty years, if it's not protected?

Just over two decades back, we rejoiced as one president declared 1.9 million acres surrounding our restaurant as the Grand Staircase-Escalante National Monument. And less than a year ago, we mourned as another president shrank its boundaries by more than half. Now a foreign company has bought rights to mine the land—despite the fact that the updated management plan for the newly amputated monument has not yet been approved nor the pending lawsuits resolved.

All my life, I have fought to preserve wilderness for the sake of wilderness, but my fight is no longer about that. We're talking now about survival—ours and that of the plants and animals and habitats under siege by runaway human destruction. Saving our common home will only happen if we preserve large, intact ecosystems in which whole communities of species, including humans, can flourish. And only if every one of us cares, engages, and takes action.

Today, as I celebrate Edward Abbey's fifty years of inspiring people to speak and act on behalf of Utah's redrock country, a passage of his runs through my mind like a daily mantra. These are the words I reflect on, the words that help me muster more love, more communal spirit, just when my heart wants to give way to anger:

This is a remote place indeed, far from the center of the world, far from all that's going on. Or is it? Who says so? Wherever two humans are alive, together, and happy, there is the center of the world. You out there, brother, sister, you too live in the center of the world, no matter where or what you think you are.

We all deserve to feel that we're at the center of the world, but the center cannot hold for much longer. The planet is heating up, changing faster than living things can adapt, disrupting natural systems and human cultures at an alarming speed.

We have a moral imperative to save wild places—not for ourselves, but for the creatures that inhabit them, the indigenous peoples whose forebears made their homes there, and, lastly, for the generations to come, who will need a just land ethic in order to thrive. It's up to us to be the ancestors who give those who follow what they will surely need.

It won't be easy, but we're unafraid, and we know where to start. Many hard battles have been won, many seemingly irreconcilable disputes resolved, over a shared meal. At the table, alchemy can occur. At the table, we can be transformed into better versions of ourselves—more civil, more communal, more sustainable.

So come to the table. Let us sit, *all* of us. Let

us eat good food, and raise a glass to Abbey, and ponder where we've been and how we proceed. For the desert wilds that Abbey knew—really, the nation he knew—is no longer.

It is indeed a new season in the wilderness.

—Blake Spalding

Former backcountry caterer and professional river chef Blake Spalding is co-owner of the award-winning Hell's Backbone Grill & Farm in Boulder, Utah, and co-author of two books, This Immeasurable Place: Food and Farming from the Edge of Wilderness *and* With a Measure of Grace: The Story and Recipes of a Small Town Restaurant

The wind

was cleansing the bones.
They stood forth silver and necessary.
It was not my body, not a woman's body,
it was the body of us all.

—Anne Carson, "The Glass Essay"

AUTHOR'S INTRODUCTION

Is this hell or heaven? Or is that the wrong question entirely?

You were laid under, elsewhere. Some have broken back and bank to find the remains but they miss the glorious, garish point: the haunt of you, the same sky.

This is hypothetical. I never leave where I always was. This is the place, after all. Never trek, seek, dig. No gold, the bones of you. If I had, I'd have gone for the skull.

This is also visceral. And here they come. In waves, in heaves, in rippled stone. Let's get this over with. There's work to do.

Between land and sky, in the liminal, a figure. Vague, hovering between forms: it drops, incarnate.

Into the rancorous red.

THE FIRST MORNING

Hey, Mr. Abbey, can you hear me down there? This yolk of sun has broken on a horizon sawed in two by saguaros and I've hopscotched my way through crypto and cacti, sidestepped a sidewinder, and given two middle fingers to an Air Force jet that buzzed me while my pants were down to pee on the playa. And now I'm squatting graveside in this lower Sonoran desert that is your resting place—a desert that has, thank the horned gods, not succumbed to the *Mad Max* lunacy in Moab.

We should talk. About the redrock country of Utah. *Desert Solitaire* was published fifty years ago this year, and as timeless as that book is, things are changing in ways even your prescient, nimble mind could not have imagined.

I'm going to sit here a minute and take in the surroundings. This is a desert more soft and yielding than those of southern Utah, one less feverish in color, less tortuous in form. It's a bit easier to

breathe here, isn't it? This place doesn't excite—
not the way canyon country does—the extremes
in our nature. And it holds the whole of the bor-
derlands—both sides—denying our tendency
toward sharp stark divisions and dumbed-down
dualities. So it's interesting, Mr. Abbey, that you
chose here, to lie *in situ*—given your aversion to
immigration. Then again, maybe you wanted to
return to Arches for a perennial season—but the
park's tumescent popularity dissuaded. After all,
you predicted rightly that the solitude you found
there once upon a time was a much-diminished
resource; if it was going, going, it's now nearly gone.
In Arches, your bones could not possibly turn to
dust in silence.

And that's why I am here today. To talk to you
about solitude. Both the lack of it and the need.
You see, it's getting pretty crowded, even in Utah,
where public lands once felt infinite. I wonder if
we know anymore what your definition of the word
even means—the feeling that is not loneliness but
"loveliness and a quiet exaltation."

So I hope you'll come up and sit with me.
For we must chew on this notion of what solitude
was, and now is. I'd suggest a walk—knowing we'd
both love to roam under this honeycomb of sky
that drips early morning gold onto spindly arms
of ocotillo, through the pale pink translucence of
jackrabbit ears. But I'm guessing that's a lot to ask

at this point, given your twenty-nine-year repose. Why don't we just sit, dig our heels into these still-cool volcanic ball bearings that masquerade as soil. I promise to seek some semblance of restraint. It won't be easy. The questions, the concerns—they threaten to rush from my body like a river freed from a blown-up dam.

Tell you what. Let's start with what is panoramic, and political. How about I rant for a bit, before working down to what is personal. And then we keep going. By nightfall, let's hope we hit bedrock—that naked, common ground.

By the way, I covered my tracks. If word got out, the GPS plot points would be posted on the Internet (long story, that) and you'd never know another moment of posthumous peace. Rest assured I got here by stealth, and now I'm sweaty, squatted, and waiting on the parched, prickly kind of land we both love. The shadows of vultures cut across my skin. They think I'm dead but never have I been so alive! Because despite what seems like increasingly dark times for the planet, these wild places persist. Places that exfoliate our neuroses. That refuse to coddle our compulsions. That remind us, in these times of profound greed, what we really need.

About Moab: you can probably imagine the jacked-up monster trucks, maybe even the Razors—these golf carts on steroids, the least sexy form of transportation known to man. But I bet you can't fathom the BASE jumpers—that's right, people now don shiny, baggy disco suits and leap off the tallest red cliffs like flying squirrels. There are also beefed-up all-terrain bikes that can circle the White Rim in a day, if you've got the quads for the job. And those delicious, hidden swimming holes in Millcreek Canyon? Some days the Bureau of Land Management has to close off access—because several hundred people are already writhing in them amid a thick scrim of sunscreen, Jaeger, and Red Bull. The entire city—plus the surrounding valley, Behind the Rocks, and beyond—emits an ever-present belch of engines. They shine Lycra and sweat caffeine. As for Arches—no matter where you stand in the park, you can hear the steady roar of it all. Everywhere you look there are these hyped-up, tricked-out, uber-fit, machine-like humans that pump, grind, climb, soar, and scramble through the desert so fast they're just a muscled blur. The land's not the thing, it's the buzz.

So there's work to be done. Our public lands—the West's de facto wilderness, its national parks and monuments—they are endangered in ways we never conceived of. Utah is in the worst shape—so many of its incomparable wildlands were protected within two of the nation's newest national monuments but our so-called Commander-in-Chief has filleted each one, leaving only the stark bones in custody. This dismemberment of the Bears Ears and Grand Staircase-Escalante, two places you knew and loved, represents the largest maiming of public lands' protection in the nation's history.

This means the green light is brighter than ever for the usual suspects of industry and motorized yahoo-ism, but the land is threatened by our ilk, the muscle-powered outdoor wanderers, too. Which is to say you, Mr. Abbey, may have developed whole fleets—generations' worth—of desert defenders, but now they're out there en masse, bumping into one another on the very ground on which you taught them to go lightly and alone. They are as much the problem as they are the solution, and it's hard to know how we don't divvy that down the middle, into us and them, right and wrong.

Your headstone says, "No Comment," but I'm hoping to discuss what we do next. You should know up front that I'm admiring, but not starstruck. You got some things right, but you got other things wrong. Like calling the desert "Abbey's country." Can you imagine, in my own book about Utah, if I had called it "Amy's country"? I could have justified it; my family has been there for seven generations and counting. Yet even with such credentials the clan of my surname doesn't get to call it *ours*—because it's all stolen property: whatever the forefathers didn't snatch from the region's Native Americans on one occasion, they took from

Mexico on another. But that's what the white man does. He comes in after the fact and lifts his leg on someone else's turf. You, sir, were no different.

Another thing: there'll be no chumminess today. I won't be calling you Ed, or Cactus Ed—although your fans do. They have good reason for assuming familiarities. When *Desert Solitaire* was published in 1968, you crowbarred open the American consciousness and the red raw desert strode right in. Like a cocklebur caught in a coyote's tail, you went with it—indistinguishable from all the convoluted canyons, scoured-out washes, mesas tiered like wedding cakes, mercurial creeks, rasping whiskers of bunchgrass, and the obsidian objections of ravens. There were also those geologic, gymnastic backbends—your beloved arches.

The New Yorker called your book an "American masterpiece." And sure enough, by the time the ragweed, dust, and scree of those essays settled, all of what you had to say took up some serious psychic real estate. You, Mr. Abbey, still lurk there. Like Hitchcock shuffling through his own film, one might not even notice you. But you're present all right, even as you bask in the director's chair. *Desert Solitaire* framed the American West through your lens, and so we see through the glass brightly: the Utah desert is not just a place to explore, not just a resource to exploit. It is a body—both politic and erotic. In every way it's scandalous.

Your claiming of Utah's desert outback taught an entire nation what it means to be in collective possession of a place. At the same time you taught us that one's interest in national lands is not a given—although the idea of it certainly is. It is only truly ours after we have gotten out of the car and wandered far enough off the trail to get lost and use up our last drop of water. Only after we've been out enough times—to draw blood, fry skin, write eulogies, pull stakes, see ghosts, and duct tape a flapping sole—should we feel in possession of them. But those of us who have done our time out there know this is the mirage, the trick of light on water that is actually scoured sand. It's the rough country, after all, that's in possession of us and not the other way around.

Look, it's early. But I've primed the old Coleman and the coffee is on.

SOLITAIRE

I'm caffeinated now, and pacing around the mound of grit heaped over what's left of you. The sky is a primrose, blooming far beyond the margins of this place, this state, this nation. A sky that shows us how not to crouch too tightly over what we claim as ours. That reminds us how to reach for, and touch, what is Other.

Circling back to the notion of informalities: I just can't. Hence the *Mister*. I'd like to keep some boundaries between us and a bit of decorum is good for that. Precautions must be taken because, as I packed for this journey, our mutual friend and iconic bookseller Ken Sanders reminded me that it wasn't just that women hurled themselves at you—you did plenty of your own hurling, too. Sure enough, a few months before you passed away, my mother drove to Sam Weller's Zion Bookstore in downtown Salt Lake City, where she stood in line for you to sign a copy of *The Fool's Progress*, which she gave to me for Christmas that year. You were nearly dead, but you hit on her. This was despite the fact that she'd read nothing you'd written. Nor was she one to wander through the desert outback. Apparently, you knew how to travel between topographies.

Another mutual friend, Charles Bowden— god rest his seared, singular soul—was a known womanizer, too. And for both of you, much has been made of this, and perhaps unfairly. Meaning you weren't exceptional—in this way, anyway. Men juggling multiple women is a common and long-standing tradition in the West, if not the world. Some of my ancestors were polygamists, as was John Singer, the man who fixed our television before dying in a shoot-out over homeschooling his kids. And a girl from a similar arrangement beat the ever-loving shit out of me on the play-ground the year before she was taken out of school to be married. We were in sixth grade at the time.

But things are changing on this front too. While you've been underground, rubbing elbows with grubs and worms, a new narrative has been in the works. For instance, there's now this thing called #metoo. (It's used for a type of brief, mass communication called "tweeting," which in this case has nothing to do with your beloved canyon wren, or any other bird for that matter.) The rules of engagement between men and women—even when consent is mutual—have been seriously upset. No one is sure of how we are to deal with each other now, but however it shakes out, I'm pretty sure you won't like it. You don't get to gawk at co-eds anymore—not without consequence. And it's no longer charming to describe us as rosy-cheeked skinny dippers—even if Katie Lee considered it a compliment.

This is not to say that I'm some shrill, ball-biting feminist with a bone to pick out of your saltbush beard. Nor am I implying we neuter or tie a tourniquet around our time together today. That would be like smothering this desert with black top, concrete, and a strip mall—but come to think of it, things here, around your grave, aren't as peaceful as this still morning would have me believe. Did you know that in the last few years at least ten thousand miles of renegade roads have been gouged into the surrounding wilderness? Not by recreational motorheads, like those in Moab. But by the United States Border Patrol. Its agents know no limits, when it comes to sniffing out tens of thousands of desperate Latinx people—only to turn them back toward the desperation. That is, if they're not indefinitely held against their will in encampments far too similar to Hitler's. The patrollers even seek and destroy the food and water caches left for the border-crossers by bleeding-heart types. This cruel effort ensures that many will perish out here, halfway between two worlds—worlds even this *desierto* cannot fuse.

~

Here, in this place where you asked to be buried on the sly, I guess it's fair to say that its solitude is an illusion. Come to think of it, you were rarely solitary in Arches. There were cattle round-ups with *caballeros*, there was barroom banter with yellowcake miners, and there were rivers run with friends. And when you were working in that trailer, scribbling away in those notebooks the desert's details that would become a bible for the desert brethren—there was a wife. There were children. And there were other women. I know it's a device, writing as though one were alone when in fact one is not. And it worked. Everyone who read that book took to the desert solo. Self included. When I first read *Desert Solitaire*, I was single and free. It was easy to follow suit. But now that I have been a working mother wrangling a special-needs child in a complicated and congested world—my definition of solitude has changed. What was once a necessity is now a luxury, and I cannot often afford it.

Which reminds me, I've been wondering about a line from that book of yours: "If we could learn to love space as deeply as we are now obsessed with time, we might discover a new meaning in the phrase *to live like men*."

I get the part about space and time. Every cell in my body would trade the latter for the former.

But the phrase that you chose to italicize . . . what did you mean, "to live like men"? Of course you meant we should quit racing like lab rats toward sugar, to fill every moment with tributes to all things temporal. And of course, you meant let's not fill every acre with reminders of our species. But were you also contemplating our urge to fill the other side of the bed or the unclaimed stool in a bar?

I'm with you, on forsaking time. On embracing space. But while we're at it, let's figure out why we cling to the contrary.

And for parity's sake, let's find out what it means to live like women. Or perhaps we should say, let's find how women like to live. I don't think we've ever been asked that question. The results could be revolutionary. Evolutionary. We might become a new species entirely.

THE SERPENTS OF PARADISE

Would you be kind enough to tell me about that first morning in Arches, when you woke up and stepped outside your tiny, tin abode and saw such vacancy? I can only imagine how wondrous that was—to see the place so obscenely, unabashedly devoid of human sign.

How your eyes must have watered and squinted, to take it all in—the vast cosmos of redfins and buttes, the intergalactic silver-green valleys, the black holes of slot canyons and alcoves where measures and dimensions no longer compute. You understood, even then, how it all would be harmed by a nation obsessed with a narrow and isolated concept of progress, not unlike the sex addict's belief that climax matters more than communion. The emblem of such a mindset remains in those stakes thrust into the ground and tied with little orange and red flags that flutter and beckon with a perverted promise of profit, no matter what the cost. But as you said, *teamwork* is what made

America what it is today! The survey crews pounded in stakes. We did our part and pulled them out. We cut the bright ribbons, too. While you hid them under rocks, I stuck them in a rucksack. Yours lined the nest of a pack rat; mine were pulled out years later and braided into my daughter's hair.

One by one, plots of public land have been leased to, then plundered by, the highest bidder. Few places are safe—and while the lands contained within Arches are off-limits, for now, the park's viewshed is not. Imagine looking through Delicate Arch: La Sal Mountains in the background and a Mars-like mesa in the fore, where the footwork of dinosaurs can still be fingered, a kind of earth braille by which to read the poetry of prehistory. Now imagine the thumper trucks, the earthmovers, the drill rigs, moving in, ready to ravage. There'll be the plunge and spurt of now-liquefied ancient creatures who laid tracks here so long ago. You won't be surprised that this is allowed, even so near to this park—one of the crown jewels of this nation, of the world. Nor will you be shocked that the latest Department of Energy secretary has called any shift away from the extraction and use of fossil fuels "immoral." In the desert, God and gasoline are still worshipped in equal measures.

Which brings me to another red flag, one whipping so wildly in the hot dry wind that even your smart skull will spin: exponential explosions of human population, ravenous for fossil fuels, harbor a hunger so serious that it dwarfs all other human dependencies combined. This is changing the atmosphere by holding heat hostage in the sky. The Natural Resources Defense Council reports that unless we curb atmosphere-altering emissions, average temperatures will likely rise by ten degrees Fahrenheit over the next century. In the last twenty years, Antarctica has lost about 134 billion metric tons of ice per year, which will cause sea levels to swell several meters over the next hundred years or so. Melting glaciers, early runoff, and severe droughts will cause more dramatic water shortages and spark bigger, more frequent wildfires throughout the American West. Forests, farms, and cities will face troublesome new pests, heat waves, heavy downpours, and increased flooding. Agriculture and fisheries will be much diminished, and many plant and animal species are already being driven into nonexistence. Allergies, asthma, and infectious diseases are on the rise, due to higher levels of air pollution and deadly pathogens. Deer ticks, which transmit the devastating Lyme disease and other illnesses, are predicted to expand their range by seventy percent in the next century. The United States makes up just four percent of the world's population, and yet we produce sixteen percent of all global CO_2 emissions—as much as the European Union and India (which occupy third and fourth place, while China is first) combined. In cumulative emissions over the past 150 years, America is still number one, by far.

To this, Mr. Abbey, you might say, "Good. Thin the herds of humans! Toughen our hides and let us simplify, for Earth's sake!"

That's all fine and good, but up north, starving polar bears totter on ice chunks the size of coffee tables, while here in the Southwest, their black cousins forget to hibernate. Thirty out of the eighty known populations of desert bighorn sheep have died out, due to lack of forage directly attributed to drought, and entire aspen communities—the trees of which are the tentacles of one miraculous being—are too thirsty to withstand elk browsing on their saplings and beetles burrowing into their trunks. And without snow, the snowshoe hare's winter coat, once his camouflage, now makes him easy pickings.

Like all good addicts, we are choosing to die rather than to withdraw. And with us we are taking down every other living thing—the hoary bat, the pike minnow, the purple sage. Every filament of grass, every piñon nut, every small continent of lichen.

There's another red flag, and while it pales in comparison to the problems of the planet, it's waving here today. That's why I am keeping with

formalities and putting this table between us. The
desert is such a turn-on, the way it slides across
the skin and pricks the senses—even when things
feel apocalyptic. We turn ruddy, bestial. Appetites
are aroused. I'm not into much-older men, even
famous ones who have been a force in my life—but
still our conversation might veer toward seduction.
It always does, when our kind is out here, licking
the salt rings off our lips so we can better kiss the
ground. And then, despite all warnings and previously suffered consequences, I'm all in. In over
my head, that is.

Let me explain this by way of a climbing
metaphor, since that was how, for years, I got my
rocks off—pun unintended, but there you are. To
enter into the thick of an amorous encounter is a
bit like pulling off a sketchy move on an exposed
cliff band: there comes the move that cannot be
reversed. One becomes committed when com-
mittal was never part of the plan. This happens a
lot, because I never find the right route, the path
of least resistance. Not until after the damage,
so much damage, has been done. Not the kind
left behind by hurricane gales out of Baja, or the
sudden rush of a flash flood—both natural pro-
cesses of erosion. I'm talking about assault that
is both anatomical and emotional in its toll: the
way front-loaders and road graders and dirt bikes
strip away the red bustiers of buttes, the black

lace stockings of desert crusts, and the dazzling green garters of lizards. That kind of toll is what I mean. The kind from which neither heart nor body recovers.

Or do they? You had five wives. I had three husbands. Was it like this for you, the collateral damage after having taken lovers and secured them as spouses, only to let them go again? Or were women like the snake coiled beneath the steps of your trailer—good, easy company as long as you didn't move too fast or get too close? I'm not out to bust you on this; I truly am curious if we are headed the same way on this trail, or if we're coming at it from opposite directions. For me, I came to believe that love *in* the desert was unlike love *for* the desert: it was not only unsustainable, but unattainable, too. A trick of light where really there was only ever shadow.

And yet, there is this new man, unlike any other. He does not cramp my need for space and silence. Nor I, his. There is no push-pull between the coming together and the going separate ways for a spell. Everything ambles with ease, like a wide-open channel of river.

Those close to me are skeptical. With good reason. But our mutual friends say that your fifth wife, with whom you stayed until the end, was, at last, the beloved. Indeed, Clarke is an incredible woman. Do you ever wonder how it would have been, to have found that one with whom we can stay, earlier in our lives? The way we found the desert?

I strayed, once. Badly. Why, I wonder, were we willing to exact so many casualties?

Maybe we were late-bloomers—moonflowers who refused, as you put it, to unfurl while "the sun roared its savage and holy light, its fantastic music in the mind." Maybe we needed the sky as dark-soft as the background in a velvet Elvis painting so we could dodge our species' tendency to burn daylight, and each other, right down to white ash.

Can we love, and be loyal to, what remains?

CLIFFROSE AND BAYONETS

There are still dregs of French roast, although they're now cold. Which is just as well, because that morning sun has set the soil ablaze, along with my skin. I'm still here at the table and looking at your vacant chair, Mr. Abbey. And while I pick cholla barbs out of my ankles, let me offer up another passage for your consideration:

> [L]ife not crowded upon life as in other places but scattered abroad in sparseness and simplicity, with a generous gift of space for each herb and bush and tree . . . so that the living organism stands out bold and brave and vivid against the lifeless sand and barren rock.

Bold and brave and vivid. I wanted to inhabit those qualities, to know myself as a specimen of what you referred to among desert life forms as "extreme individuation." I believed as you do—that "love flowers best in openness and freedom." Give the prickly pear and claret cup wide berth and somehow you'll appreciate their petals even more.

Those conditions were printed on my first wedding invitation—but I was thinking botanically. Then I caught Husband #1 with coke-crusted nostrils, making out with a woman from my EMT class. I was nineteen and we were at Moab's Old City Park, dancing to a reggae band after a day of climbing. Clearly he saw your words in a different light.

Post-divorce, I tried to date casually. My community—climbers, hikers, river-runners, and canyoneers—they nicknamed me "Miss Catch and Release." It was intended to be pejorative. Double standards, even among the enlightened desert rats, still exist. When I finally tried to commit again was the one time I was disloyal. My handle stuck.

I was young, but, remember, I'm a Utah girl. If you want to get laid, you get married, or get labeled a trawler. So it took awhile—three more decades—to see that I chose men who believed they flowered best in a more open, free arrangement than what a committed partnership required. Men not unlike you. Or our friend Bowden. I miss that man like I miss my own deceased father—who, come to think of it, also played the field. In Abbey's country, that kind of infidelity is encouraged, even celebrated—if you're male.

But that's the rub! You guys have always waxed lyrical about the isolation, the independence, but the truth is you couldn't handle the wide-open between organisms, the sparseness of desert society. You were always seeking much closer, more carnal, companions.

As was I. As were your fans. They swallowed your solitude hook whole but they'll come out of the dry-rotted, termite-riddled woodwork to congregate, let me tell you. A cult following if there ever was one. Awhile back, there was a literary festival in Moab to honor you and all your books. Doug Peacock was there, Craig Childs, and others. The town was awash with your readers. Craig and I were teaching a writing workshop on scene and one of our students was so much a fan of *Desert Solitaire* that he had dropped off the New York Stock Exchange for good and headed west in a tricked-out camper van. He had quit the tie and suits, sworn off women and pricey single-malts. And he'd taken up yoga to cure his Type AAA personality and urbanitis. In class, as each person read aloud their desert writing, this guy—decked out in new Prana separates and matching Chacos—would leap to his feet and gleefully pretzel himself into the pose that reflected some key aspect of the scene: downward dog for the mention of coyotes and tree pose for cottonwoods. Cliffrose was his lotus. Bayonets of cactus quills were taken up in warrior. But it was wheel pose he loved best, because it looked like one of your arches. He contained the desert, your words, his passions—in his own body. It's not a stretch to say that you salvaged the man's soul.

My tree pose is a very old juniper that stood along a creek bed below the house on a mesa east of the La Sal Mountains, a house I once shared with my daughter's father. An old fruit tree had grown entwined with the juniper's tornado-like trunk and limbs. It was so sensual, that arboreal union—a duet both wild and domestic. We shared the fruit with the resident black bears. My kid plucked her first apple from those branches. One day, when Ruby was six, we walked down to the creek bottom, apple-picker and bucket in tow. A bulldozer had plowed the two trees and it was evident how they went down, the twists twisting more and more until each tree splintered in half. And yet with unbroken boughs the two of them still clung to one another like lovers having leaped off the sinking *Titanic* into a cold dark sea. Ruby ran forward but I hung back, wanting my daughter to form her own feelings about what had been done to a place that she knew as home, trees that she knew as family. She turned red with rage, then wet-gray with sorrow and tears. Next she wiped her face and dragged rocks, logs the size of her body, and a coil of old rusted barbwire—anything she could find—into the paths of the parked and vacant machines. For a finale, she kicked the big tires with every ounce of force she could muster.

"Mommy," she asked later, still livid and grieving. "Is there a word for what I did today?"

Monkey-wrenching didn't quite say it. In that amber autumn sun that pressed through the sky like cider, it was a bold, brave, and vivid word, but it didn't convey the whole of it—the love and the loss.

I kneeled and put my arms around her tiny waist and ran my fingers through the auburn tumbleweed on her head.

"Fidelity," I said.

POLEMIC: INDUSTRIAL TOURISM AND THE NATIONAL PARKS

You taught us at the get-go that the problem we were up against wasn't just coal mining and uranium tailings. It was tourism, too. Like you, I was a park ranger in Utah, although my job happened amid limestone instead of sandstone, at Timpanogos Cave National Monument, just south of Salt Lake City. Once, on the trail, I caught Boy Scouts smashing a rattlesnake into pulp. Another day, in the cave, I caught a Japanese tourist breaking off and pocketing a stalactite as souvenir.

In case you've completely dispensed with the concept of time, I'll let you know that the one hundredth anniversary of America's National Park System was just two years ago. That year, over 330 million people visited the lands within the system's protection. The next year, Donald Trump leaped from the stage of a reality TV show and landed in the Oval Office. According to the National Parks Conservation Association, here's what our current president did to our national parks and monuments during his first year of office:

- Issued a hiring freeze on National Park Service staff, despite parks already having ten percent fewer rangers and other staff than they did a few years ago, and despite record-breaking crowds.
- Repealed the Clean Water Rule, which provides protections for many streams, wetlands, and other waterways that are essential to the health of national parks and monuments.
- Issued a sweeping executive order on "energy independence" with numerous negative consequences for public lands. It mandated:
  o The Department of the Interior to review standards that protect more than forty national parks from the impacts of oil and gas drilling inside their boundaries.
  o The Environmental Protection Agency to withdraw and rewrite rules mandating that power plants limit carbon dioxide.
  o Federal agencies to no longer consider the effects of climate change when deciding whether to issue permits for fossil fuel production.
  o Both the EPA and BLM to delay enacting standards to reduce methane pollution from oil and gas operations.
- Repealed the Clean Power Plan, which reduced

emissions from energy development and improved conservation measures to combat climate change, the number one threat to national parks.

- Rescinded an NPS directive to use comprehensive, science-based management practices to combat climate change, biodiversity loss, invasive species, pollution, and other threats to national parks. By repealing the measure, the agency is removing scientific considerations from its management practices.

- Issued an executive order calling on the Department of the Interior to consider granting energy developers access to areas previously closed to offshore oil and gas drilling, threatening coastal parks and marine wildlife. It also orders the Department of Commerce to refrain from designating or expanding any national marine sanctuary until it is evaluated for energy resource potential, and to review any marine sanctuaries or monuments established over the last ten years.

- Signed proclamations removing protections from more than two million acres of national monument land at Bears Ears and Grand Staircase-Escalante National Monuments, opening up previously protected land to potential drilling, mining, and logging.

ROCKS

You won't be surprised to hear that in Utah nearly every trail has been widened. The location of every petroglyph publicized. And so many sheer, patina-coated walls are now studded with shiny climbing bolts and fixed anchors—all of which are inserted with motorized drills.

I'll confess that, in my twenties, I bolted a few rock walls on BLM lands. One line was a perfect *V*, either side of which contained gently folded lips of flesh-colored sandstone. There was a deep runnel, made by water, right down the middle. It was the most vulvar, un-phallic rock formation I'd ever seen. I bolted it. Climbed it and rated the difficulty. I also named it "God Between Their Lips," the title of a book written by my favorite professor of all things feminist and theological, who taught in the women's studies program at the University of Utah. In my memory, the man who belayed me for the first ascent didn't feel comfortable with the route name. This was the man I betrayed, a man with whom I fought on our wedding night because he didn't think Susan B. Anthony deserved to appear on US currency. A few years later, when a guide-book to this particular climbing area came out, the route had been renamed, downgraded, and its first ascent claimed by some guy from St. George. Maybe this serves me right for having taken a drill to the rock in the first place.

And while you know these next thoughts, I'm going to say them anyway: the minute there is a line drawn around these lands, a sign staked on their behalf, the masses come running. They come at full tilt, with their mountain bikes, ropes, and GoPros—these are cameras they strap to their heads to film the thrill of the moment so it lasts a lifetime. Sure, they wear their eco-fleece and they mostly bury their poop and stay on the trails, but still we're talking about droves of people—and yes, here in mid-rant I haven't forgotten that I am one of those folks too. Except I am not very sporty, or gear-intensive—not anymore. Now I just want to wander off the beaten path in my torn-up jeans. I want to get lost, I mean so totally turned around that I see the land without preconception. As if for the very first time. But with every new human added to our population, every new guide-book written, and every new place protected and promoted, it's getting harder to have a wild and reckless reckoning that has nothing to do with recreation. And entertainment. That has everything to do with sensation. And salvation.

Sure, monuments and parks also keep things out—the drill rigs and ATVs. At least they used to, pre-Trump. But back to the elephant in the desert—*us*. I cannot help but wonder how the relationship between the desert and me, just one of so many bodies in need of a getaway, could possibly be, at this point anyway, symbiotic. Aren't we, too—if only by our sheer numbers, our hunger for a break from our crazed, compressed lives—blindly careening toward our own release without knowing the body-that-is-the-desert, simply as it is? Something beyond a pornographic projection of our own aesthetic and athletic appetites?

You and I, we are complicit. We took ranger jobs not because we wanted to show people the places we loved deeply and privately. No, we took those jobs for a more selfish reason: so we could make bank while spending our days in the wild. We winced when folks asked if they could see the place in less than an hour and we seethed when new graffiti was gauged into the rocks. We picked up trash, pointed to porta-potties, then gritted our teeth when we had to say, "Thank you and come again."

It bought us both space and time. All the while, we secretly hoped that *some* of them, *any* of them, would fall in love—and madly. That they'd swear fealty. Because if people came to care about the way the air shimmers when the rabbitbrush shrugs off the heat and sends it rolling across the slickrock, the way the antelope bolt like lightning unleashed from a squalid sky—maybe we'd stand a prayer of a chance to save the places we treasure from those who would take some quick and dirty form of amusement over poetry, beauty, and wonder.

Be safe. Play only in clockwise, conchoidal directions. We'll have to do more than *have fun* together.

COWBOYS AND INDIANS

Mid-morning now, and hellishly hot, so I've donned a long-sleeved shirt and my grandfather's greasy, brow-beaten Resistol hat. He was the real deal, you know. Ran five hundred head of cattle in the high desert country of southern Idaho. I mention this because you and I seem to share the acquaintance of stockmen and a fondness for moving through rough country on horseback. I don't know—perhaps rounding up herds of cows via equines gave us both the excuse to feel a greater sense of meaning and purpose out there, to deem our place in the desert as somehow more worthy than the tourists'. Neither of us ever wanted to just pass through.

Whatever the motives, I think that we both understand the "other side" of this public lands debate—by which I mean the self-proclaimed old-timers, the rural folk. Which is, of course, not the other side at all—not even the likes of Cliven Bundy and the guys who took over the Malheur

Wildlife Refuge in Oregon. Most of today's environmental groups won't agree, but you might, when I say that sometimes I vote libertarian to help break up the country's two-party gridlock, but also because I love the *idea* of what those guys did; I love the active resistance, the sticking it to institutions too large and lethargic to be effective. After all, the folks who have defied federal authority believe as you believed, that we might need the wild wooliness of the West "as a refuge from authoritarian government," and "as bases for guerilla warfare against tyranny."

The anti-federalist, Mormon part of me agrees with your words, their actions. But, for Bundy's kind, the land's not the thing either. It's another kind of buzz that has to do with big guns, big hats, and big boots. It's not the lawlessness that gets me as much as heartlessness—the way the cows go starving and the land perishes from too many large and foreign beasts on it. It's not a thing we can afford. For me, it's a matter of degrees. My grandfather, the other ranchers I've moved cows for—none of them sits on the extreme and hostile end of the spectrum. Besides, there are so few independent ranch outfits remaining they are hardly the main problem. But I'll tell you what is:

I was invited to speak at a book club in Salt Lake City, my hometown. The host's directions took me up one of the city's seven canyons to a tall iron gate, which ran across the hillside for as far as I could see. On a keypad, I entered a security code and the gate rolled open to a razed hilltop lathered in huge, shiny new homes built from whole forests of trees, steel, hewed stone, concrete, granite, and marble. The gathering was to be held in such a structure, and when I found the right one I squeezed my Subaru between the megafauna— Ford Explosions and Land Rovers—all of which sported stickers that claimed allegiance to The Nature Conservancy or Sierra Club.

I entered the host's home, which may as well have been a ski lodge, so vast and luxuriously rustic-chic it was. A table displaying imported wine, olives, cheese, grapes, and shrimp beckoned— items that traveled from farmers and vintners and fishermen to warehouses and then to the distributors, and then to Salt Lake storefronts. After these items were purchased, they were driven home— from the heart of the city to the McMansion atop this canyon. They were laid out next to recyclable paper plates, napkins, and cutlery. A blue recycling bin stood proudly at table's end to collect what could be used, in some other fashion, again.

We filled our plates and glasses and gathered in a great room fit for kings and queens. We discussed my living in and writing about rural southern Utah, among people who hate that the Feds are in charge of lands they believe to be their backyard.

At one point, a woman wrinkled her nose and said, "God, I hate all those backwoods rednecks down there. Their lifestyle is *totally* unsustainable."

The other book club members nodded and murmured in agreement.

I leaned into the fire at my back, a fire that should have been making my skin bead with sweat but instead left me lukewarm because the hearth was so absurdly large. I took in the impeccable hygiene, the curiously bright white teeth, the new hip clothes. I thought about my rural neighbors, and my own ranching relatives. All of them lived in *much*, much smaller houses than this. They grew, raised, or hunted nearly all their own food. Their cars and trucks were driven until there were three hundred thousand miles on the engines. They owned about two pairs of jeans and one pair of boots each, and they reused every piece of baling twine. Hardly ever did they use fuel to go on a "road trip," let alone commute to work or to a book club or fly in airplanes to exotic places. And the cattle they trucked to sale? They were sold to the supermarkets and restaurants the rest of us frequent, to serve as the main course for the paleo diets to which the good liberals prescribe—diets that burn way too much carbon but hey, they burn fat too—especially if we drive across town after work for a CrossFit class before heading back out to the suburbs to pump more protein into our systems so we are lean and chiseled and ready to head to the desert come Friday afternoon, where we'll camp, cook, poop, and pump our bikes amid ancient grounds where the region's Native Americans once buried their dead, gathered their wood, harvested their medicine, hunted their sustenance, and painted their prayers.

These good white liberals want monuments and wilderness to protect the places they recreate, to keep out companies that want to suck the fossil fuels out from under the sandstone. But the oil and gas will be burned by and large by *them*, to travel to Utah's public lands. And it's used by *us*—you in your big red Cadillac and me in my Toyota truck—although I've recently downgraded to a more fuel-efficient Subaru, the preferred method of transport that's most often frosted with bike, ski, and boat racks for outdoor enthusiasts across the nation.

The land and those who live off it know this arrangement breeds no symbiosis. We all want to get to, and get off on, a body corralled and commodified. Our orgasmic need for release and relief eclipses the fact that this is the living, breathing body of the Beloved—the naked desert that has been demarcated and delineated—ribbed, we believe, for our pleasure.

But you knew all this, even then—before Arches was paved and Moab became a monument to motors and muscles. You gave us warning. *Desert Solitaire* was another kind of red flag, waving wildly in the blinding, blasting wind through which we have failed to see our own tracks.

So now what? How has the land become beside the point, even as people go to such lengths there—to play on it, to make a living on it?

If we objectify, we can enjoy. To love any more deeply is to love in a way that devastates. As you said about the drowning of Glen Canyon, the most tragic of all Ophelias, "[W]e dare not think about it for if we did we'd be eating our hearts, chewing our entrails, consuming ourselves in the fury of helpless rage. Of helpless *out*rage."

We are they.

The new adventure starts now. It takes place on hazardous, heartbreaking terrain, without the contagions of carbon.

No longer can we be voyeurs, catching from scenic pullouts mere glimpses of the wild, uneven territory of our collective unconscious. The hour at hand demands that we molt all that we want and believe we know. Now we must slither—belly to stone—into the dens and burrows of our souls.

COWBOYS AND INDIANS: PART II

You'll notice that I've set out a Stanley flask. It's full of Bulleit rye—which I have no idea if you like, but I do. Next to your seat is a small cooler full of iced Coors; Ken told me it was your preferred beverage. You can toss the cans if you want, if that will get you up here; right now the least of the desert's worries is a few aluminum cylinders getting caught in the pickleweed.

Oh, and just for fun, let's load and lay on the table at the ready our sidearms—your Colt .45 and my Glock 9mm. Because we're near the border, and these days, it gets dangerous out here. I know where you'll go with that, so if I haven't made myself clear by now, it's not the migratory Mexicans who are the problem.

The man at the center of all the new trouble with Mexico and the rest of Latin America—he wants to build a wall between our southern neighbors and us. This man with Agent Orange hair and a napalm personality, who has no concept of humanity or nature, is worse than ten of your James G. Watts. The wall will pay homage to his wreckage. The cost will be blood and funds not his own.

Now I'm wondering if this was such a good idea, to have traveled all this way, to talk to this desiccated version of you. Because, in *The Red Caddy*, Chuck Bowden tossed one of your "verbal hand grenades," as he called them, which is this: "Stop those Mexicans at the border, give 'em each a Winchester 94 and a case of ammo, and then send them home equipped to solve their own problems." The most offensive and dangerous president in US history being hell-bent on building a wall between Mexico and the United States is something you might actually *approve* of. Does this mean you might not approve of the Bears Ears becoming our nation's newest national monument—an effort led not by great white environmental groups, but rather an inter-tribal coalition of Ute, Navajo, Hopi, and Zuni leaders? Might you have cheered on the president's undoing of it?

Hold onto yer hat. This shit's getting complicated. Maybe we better empty our rounds, because you and I might be headed for a showdown.

WATER

Let me begin again. With something we can agree on. So, Mr. Abbey, please come up and sit. I've gone ahead and cracked you a cold one for the occasion.

Consider this: the wall, which would be built not far from here, would not only keep out people but also jaguars, which have only *just begun* to pad their way back into Arizona after a long and grim hiatus. And did you know there is a herd of wild bison that travels daily, back and forth between the two countries? They graze on the American side, where the grass is, and then water on the Mexican one—at the only hole for miles. With a wall in place, they will die. The same holds true for the Sonoran pronghorn. The javelina, ocelot, and wolves.

Earth first. Be not an atheist but an eartheist. Hell, yes! But what about the humans? They aren't a problem that's likely to go away—not soon, anyway. I know that you and the poet Jeffers were both of the mind that you'd rather dispatch our species than hawks or snakes, but on an evening in Arches, when a visitor pushed you to sharper thinking, you discovered that you were "not opposed to mankind, but only to man-centeredness." Fair enough. At the heart of this whole planetary demise is the issue of population—and that does in fact seem to be a selfish gesture. Yet here I am, once again: culpable. As are you, for having brought children into an already crowded world.

I don't know what to do about this, because population reduction won't happen without some sort of exertion of control over women's bodies, their sexuality. You can guess by now how that sits with me. Besides, my thirteen-year-old daughter, Ruby—she loves animals beyond measure. She's given up eating meat, adopted a desert tortoise, and organized a fundraiser that donated hundreds of dollars of supplies for the animal rescue operation in Old La Sal. And as I've mentioned already, she has no problem with wrathful acts of resistance. I'm pretty sure at this point she won't ever be a Republican. But she's probably not a Democrat either; she's far too honest about her part in the planet's problems.

Ruby isn't worried about texting boys or applying watermelon-flavored lip gloss. She loses sleep over pollution, development, extinctions, climate change, and school shootings, and she knows it's her generation's job to change the terrible version of the world we're handing down to them. But she is game for the task in ways you and I never were, so I won't feel too guilty about having produced such a kid. My girl is cut from the same cloth as Malala Yousafzai, Julia Butterfly Hill, and Emma González. And the women who started the Black Lives Matter and Standing Rock movements. I don't know how these female activists and the causes they champion sit with you. Meaning I'm not sure how deep your chauvinism and bigotry really run. Perhaps, in your mind, such attitudes are, like solitude, literary devices.

Ruby is the face of a hopeful, sustainable future where an informed and active citizenry rebuilds at the edges of where the wild things are—and, if she has any say, where they will remain. Yet she'd never turn away from a human in need. She's the kid who sells half her product at her lemonade stand and pours free drinks for the homeless people passing by. She shares her earnings with them, so they can buy a hot meal or a shower.

"I have what I need," she says, "and that's enough."

It's true. By choice, the kid owns two pairs of shoes.

THE HEAT OF NOON:
ROCK AND TREE AND CLOUD

It's twelve o'clock, Mr. Abbey, and somewhere in your beloved Arches is a hiker sporting ExOfficio garb with an SPF of fifty, a CamelBak pack, and Merrell boots. He is waving his red bandana at anything flying overhead. He needs help because he drank a half-dozen quad-shot lattés in order to work sixty-plus hours before a red-eye to Salt Lake City, and then a rental car drive to Moab, where he imbibed too much desert pale ale, and the next morning, that is *this* morning, he forgot to tighten the lid on the CamelBak bladder. At some point, hours ago, he veered off the beaten park path into the back of beyond, where he learned he has lost all his water. He's shaky now, and seeing double. He needs a rescue—which he can luckily summon on his cell phone. This means grids of volunteers on foot, droves of good ol' boys on ATVs, and helicopters buzzing overhead. Now the whole desert is a shit-show just because this guy forgot to attend to the details of his fancy, over-designed gear. And still he's not remotely as fucked as the border-crossers. Especially the children who've been torn away from their parents.

Did I mention he belongs to The Wilderness Society?

This man. His circumstances. I am catching him at a bad time, releasing him as a mockery for you to see. In this way, I share your so-called misanthropy—and it's likely arrogant on both our parts. Because we have found ourselves lost and delirious—you in Havasu, me in Dark Canyon, to name just one instance each. No doubt there was a point when we'd have conceded to a rescue—if we could have hailed one.

Or not. After all, this is how we come to inhabit a place. To inhabit ourselves. This un-finding, this kind of reduction down to bone on stone, is what you and I were gunning for all along.

We are lost in a new way. And as the land fades to black we need our Hitchcock. We need him to get all eyes on the place in the frame, the whole of it. Whether the director likes it or not, that frame must be widened—made panoramic even—so as to include a herd, a horde, a half-assed happenstance of bumbling humans. Not all of them know who you are. Some worship Aron Ralston, the man who in a slot canyon cut off his own arm, which was pinned beneath a boulder.

Others idolize Dean Potter, a notorious climber and BASE jumper who in his squirrel suit flew into one of Yosemite's granite walls. Both bumbled perilously—and in Dean's case, fatally—in national parks and wilderness. What a glorious right and privilege.

Not everyone knows that these new heroes— yes, that's what our culture by and large views them as—were building off of your desert forays. The heroes themselves might not even know.

But I see you. Batting your way through the tamarisk. I'm over here, knee-deep and flailing in the quicksand. There are others, too. All of us glad to be out here. Gladder than hell to be stuck, disoriented, and thirsty. In love and alive. If only as dust in the wind.

THE MOON-EYED HORSE

The beer I've cracked for you is now flat and warm, but I'm three fingers into the rye. I'm pondering the many octaves of emotion that exist beyond that which most of us are willing to feel. Which leads me to wondering about that horse you tried to befriend. He turned his back on humanity because our kind had not been good to him. He found solace in the canyons and learned to be all that a horse is naturally *not*, which is to say he became solitary.

Your attempt to connect with the ghostly gelding was almost laughable, but no less than mine with a similar beast. I'm cutting up some cheese and an apple with my grandfather's pocket-knife—my inheritance, if you include the hat—while I tell you about my horse, who also lived alone outside of Moab.

I was losing my mind as a stay-at-home mother when my neighbor asked if I knew how to ride a horse, because she needed help moving two hundred head of Angus. As a child I was deathly allergic to horses, but I was willing to give it a try—and when she put me on her Arabian, I found I did just fine. Riding the high desert was way more fun than changing diapers, so I kept at it. And when my third marriage started heading south, I thought our mutual love for horses would save us. If #3 played cowboy to my cowgirl, perhaps we would be able to stick things out. So I got my own horse. But not just any horse.

The horse I want to tell you about wasn't gelded until he was thirteen years old—which means he was by and large still a stallion who had lived his whole life in a round pen—let out only to service the brood mares. He was badly treated. Eventually he was abandoned in Spanish Valley; his most recent owner tied him to a post where he stood in cresting summer heat for three days without food, shade, or water. The two women who run the animal sanctuary in Old La Sal, along with the local vet, saved his life.

I named him Dante. He was as red as burnished sandstone. On a dime, he could turn murderous. Around men especially, the soft lunar light in his eye could suddenly burn infernal.

At first there was not so much trust as an understanding that we'd tolerate one another as best we could; neither of us had much faith in partnerships anymore. But months later, after hundreds of hours of work in the arena, we rode out at last. He had a dominant personality but he was terrified to walk out ahead of the other horses, into the spare, sandstone world beyond fences, beyond the little patch of dirt that he'd known for years on end.

He was a flirt, too. Competed for me with Husband #3. The guy could bench press three hundred pounds at a time, but that horse managed to pin him in the back of his stall for a good twenty minutes. But toward me, he grew kind and willing. One day, on a ride with #3 and friends, I begged Dante to stand his ground when the other horses ran away with their riders. They'd been spooked by a mountain lion and everything in my horse screamed that he too, should *GO*.

But he stayed. Because I asked him to. And this brought the other horses to a stop before someone was killed. Funny how, after that moment of panicked horses racing straight at us—one dragging its unconscious rider by the boot across the ground—Dante gentled. Somehow halting the stampede helped him to reclaim his horse-ness, from which he had held himself apart. Actually, it's more accurate to say that he'd been held apart from other horses, except when they were presented as sex objects in need of servicing. He had been the worst kind of lone and rugged macho man, and then he was none of that. This, after a year of mounting Ruby's mare constantly—until her backside was raw. After rearing madly at every fencepost. After trying to clobber with his front hooves my third spouse when he came within striking distance.

Next came desert adventures like none I'd ever known—and I fell in love with the desert in a new way. It was no longer about finding the solitude, but about cultivating the relationship. Our bodies came together to encounter the landscape in which he'd suffered heat, thirst, and hunger. In which he'd nearly perished.

But Dante began to drop on the trail. I had to dive off the saddle, into the brush, to avoid being crushed. He'd shake and roll—a big, quivering mess. With my belly in the dirt and my mouth full of sand, I'd watch the red flag of him, all aflutter in the desert, warning me never to take a partner for granted.

Two vets deemed him unrideable. So I took him back to Old La Sal, to the sanctuary, where he'd never be handed off again to someone who might mistreat him. No man has ever broken my heart the way it broke on the day I gave up that horse. And walking on foot again, even in canyon country, just wasn't the same.

For a long time afterward, the journey was lonelier than ever.

DOWN THE RIVER

Look at these guns of ours, all sleek and gleaming in that now-wretched sun. Literally, they are too hot to handle. But they remind me of this other thing I want to talk about, which is why I have carried a firearm in the wild. More than once I've come too close to feeling like prey—and I don't mean for cougars, bears, or wolves.

I am a kid. My family is camping on the Green River. In the night a man enters a neighboring tent and puts a knife to the throat of a woman while her husband and children beg for her life.

I'm twenty-something. At home on the road, I travel from one climbing area to another, when another female climber goes out for a run and is taken by a man who kills women for sport.

I'm a new mother nearing my fortieth birthday. I kneel on a dirt road and try to change a flat tire when a truck full of men on meth starts circling like a shark. Brandishing the tire iron, I run at the truck and scare them away, but still, you can imagine.

All of these moments happened on public lands. While I would give every limb to have had your job in Arches—the nearest human being twenty miles away and little but a resident rattlesnake to guard the perimeter—I must say, the thought also scares me. I don't suffer from hysteria, as Freud would have you believe. In the United States, a woman is raped every two minutes and eighty-one percent of us have been sexually harassed. Meaning the vast majority of us have feared for our jobs or our lives. You might be shocked to hear that, just as you might squirm when I tell you that most mass shooters and serial killers—we have a lot of them these days—are white males.

Something has got to give. Because the thing that came to mind when I read how you floated down the river with Newcomb was the time I was on a remote stretch of a similar river when a man with needle tracks on his burned and shirtless arms stumbled out of the shadows and began to threaten my three friends and me. The strapping guys in our group escorted him out of camp and back up some old Jeep road from whence he came, but you see my point. Solitude, for women, is a different animal entirely.

I'm not trying to paint your gender to be all bad. I came to love the wild world by way of boys and men; it was they who taught me to hunt, climb, paddle, build fires, read maps, ski, and throw knives.

Of course, in the beginning, there was my father. Our first adventure in my memory took place on a dark tongue of river, in eastern Utah, just below Flaming Gorge Dam. It was Memorial Day weekend. I was eight and my sister, Paige, was six. The first morning, the weather was unseasonably cold and gray, with a damp velvet hand that was hard to shake. The spring runoff had been let loose from behind the dam; the river was fast and high. As my father shoved away from the shore, my mother expressed her doubts—which my father promptly blew off, and this wasn't the first time he'd done that. An hour later, when the high winds howled upriver and the waves rose like mythic sea creatures to greet them, his response was to whoop with glee—a feat, given that his mouth was occupied with the stub of a Swisher Sweet. He refused to put down either fishing rod or cigar to steer the boat. Not even for the big sinkhole toward which we were headed.

I was kneeling in the bow of the boat and felt a kind of awe. The latex floor of the vessel was gelatinous beneath my small bony knees, and through it, I could feel the current. I also felt the sheer force of the water as it sucked the raft up and over the swell, before it slam-dunked the boat into the dark and foreboding sinkhole. I wasn't old enough to know that my father should have turned the boat perpendicular beforehand, that coming in sideways in such a small watercraft was very poor form indeed.

I clung to the bowline and squinted as the water hit my face. My mother and sister screamed and my father grunted with a perverse pleasure. And then, just like that, the raft popped out of the hole and we were moving downstream again, and fast. My father tossed me a metal Folgers can and I bailed like mad. But my hand forgot the task—it hung suspended between the scoop and dump—because I was looking back for one last glimpse of the hole. My dad barked at me then, to keep bailing. Above the roar of the water and the wails of her youngest daughter, my mother cursed from the top of her lungs at the man she had married but would soon divorce.

Another bend in the river and wind slid the raft sideways across the water, like a knife cutting across a cake. It rammed the boat into a sheer cliff with a sharp overhang—cut from eons of water banking steadily off it. The overhang was just at head level, so my mother put out her hands to keep the edge from nailing my sister's skull. She bloodied her palms in the process. As my family sailed backwards past the take-out, my dad's paddling was at last the priority but now pointless. A man onshore saw the trouble we were in and dove into the swift water, which I recall as frothing and bottle green. He grabbed the line my father tossed but couldn't find his footing. He too was nearly swept away—until other folks on the bank rushed in and pulled to dry ground the man, the raft, and my sodden, sputtering family.

That trip ruined it for my mother and sister. Squelched the whole outdoor adventure thing. The week after, in the supermarket, my mother ran into a woman with whom she played bridge and held up her hands. I hid behind the half-full cart as my mother recounted the story, to which the woman shuddered and said how it was just like a man to put his family in that precarious position.

Here's the thing: my mom and sister stayed in camp the next day, but I got back in the boat. And when I was soaked to the bone and my lips a cadaverous shade of blue, my father finally noticed and steered the craft—this time with success—to a small beach beneath a rock alcove, where he built a fire of pale gray driftwood. As the smoke and heat rose to lick the stone ceiling overhead, hundreds of fat, black spiders dropped down from the *huecos* in the overhang. They dangled from their threads, inches from my face. I wanted to scream, with so many, so close. But I was with my dad, crouched in a cave, the fire's warmth seeping into my skin. The two of us shared a bag of waterlogged beef jerky. It was the most delicious, primal food I'd ever eaten.

In that moment, my father was my *locus Dei*.

Just as he was that night in camp, when he put a pistol to the ribs of the man holding a knife to that woman's throat. After that, for far too long, I would deify the guys who followed. And in this way, I missed what you, Mr. Abbey, described as the "rainbow-colored corona of blazing light, pure spirit, pure being, pure disembodied intelligence, *about to speak my name.*" Which means that when I was tucked under that overhang of stone as porous as a sun-bleached skeleton, spiders waving on air like prayer flags and the meat on my tongue like an offering, I failed to hear the roar of the river as the chanting monks in the temple, brothers and sisters in the tabernacle. It was the calling to enter into communion with not just one man or one god— because oh, how those two get confused. Not even with one creature—say, a horse—but with every being in the whole wide web of the world, each of us, a sacred and vital strand.

HAVASU

Now about your descent into Havasu: it sounds like my idea of a delightful trip. Especially the part where you got good and stuck in that slot and braced for a long, painful death. You called it one of the happiest nights of your life. I've had trips like that—one that left me benighted atop L'Aiguille du Midi in Chamonix, and another in Utah's Dark Canyon Wilderness, where getting lost for a night meant waking up to a roar and running for my life as a flash flood came careening around the bend.

These experiences are signs of lives well-lived. So I guess we're not much different than Aron Ralston or Dean Potter. Getting to the outer limits of oneself, even if we don't return with all our parts, even if we don't survive, is what puts us in touch with our animal selves, the place in which physical hungers sharpen but material longings lessen. At last we are in the moment where every breath, every bead of sweat, matters. Let us not forget, though, that to move through the natural world in this way is a privilege that belongs to the able-bodied, upper classes. Those well-educated, well-employed, and mobile enough. Those with the means and free time to make the trip.

Which leads me to another issue. This time with your Conradian moment in Havasu, where you delighted in "going native," a phrase that sits squarely in the same province as "Abbey's country." Now you're probably rolling your eyes down there, thinking that I'm flashing some PC badge at you, but it's so much more than that. Our kind can go primal, we can go feral, we can caterwaul, and go AWOL, but we hardly know what it means to be native to anything anymore.

You likely meant it tongue in cheek, but I hiked into Havasu Canyon the year after a Havasupai Indian killed a female tourist, stabbing her twenty-nine times. I'd carried my daughter in; the camping gear came on the backs of godawful-looking horses and mules driven by men who never smiled. While the rest of our party was out hiking one day, I took Ruby to the waterfall. Pebbles pinged around us as we waded in the aquamarine pool. Then the stones hit closer, and they were bigger. I looked up to the cliff tops, where a young local man in a Denver Broncos shirt scowled plainly at us. Being spotted didn't stop him from throwing more rocks. I scooped up Ruby and hurried back to camp—a camp so large and packed with tents and stoves it could have been a refugee settlement. Except that these were mostly white people who had paid top dollar for their gear as well as the chance to enter the only portion of Grand Canyon National Park to be commanded—if you can call it that—by a Native American government.

The rest of the village was in bad shape, and its residents cool to us, at best. I wasn't surprised, seeing as most Native American nations have been relegated to postage stamps of land and subjected to endless cycles of poverty, disease, abuse, and addiction. It wasn't until we hiked back up to the rim that I learned about the murder the year before, and how insult had added to injury. By the time I arrived, tensions were at an all-time high between tourists and residents. Since the murder, investigators had heard from women who'd been assaulted in Havasu Canyon but hadn't reported the attacks. Such cases involved young male tribal members as well as a large white man who called himself "an Indian sympathizer." He slept in the bushes and partied with the locals in an attempt to "integrate." On two separate occasions, a woman hiking alone was grabbed from behind by a man who tried to pull her off the trail; luckily, both women got away. One investigator went on record saying that women shouldn't hike alone in Havasu Canyon—it was just too dangerous.

So don't be that creepy white dude who's trying to siphon a sense of meaning and belonging off the desert's Native peoples, Mr. Abbey. They have enough troubles.

And for godssakes. Leave the women be—or you might get punched, kicked, maced, or worse. We're a little on edge these days.

THE DEAD MAN
AT GRANDVIEW POINT

A writing mentor once explained to me the difference between writing about what is personal, and what is private—the private being the stuff that should stay off the page. I'm still hopeless at discerning between the two, so it may be that I'm now getting too close for comfort. Maybe I've trespassed into the private realm and maybe that's why you still haven't made an appearance.

I could blame it on the whiskey but really, I've only hit about half the strata in this dig and still there is much to say—stuff that no one wanted to hear even a year ago, but this latest president loves pussy grabs as much as land grabs and so do many of the people who put him in power. So I'm not stopping. It's only fair that if you get to wax on about the takedown of governments and the sabotage of industry, then I should get to take my shots at patriarchy. Because that's part of the problem and one you aren't in much of a position to address.

Example: as a father, you had the privilege of going to Pack Creek for days at a time, to write in solitude. As a new mother, I *lived* at Pack Creek, across the road from Seldom Seen and the little cabin he and his wife provided for you. I was under contract to write a book. My pen was put down to breastfeed. It wasn't picked up again for years because I was always packing the car and rushing my child to Salt Lake, then to Arizona, then as far away as the Eastern Seaboard. I did this first because of an autoimmune disease and then later, all-night marathons of seizures. With my daughter there have been so many, many sleepless nights, so many close calls. I didn't keep a journal, I kept vigil.

I'm not bitter, or maybe I am. But don't think I tell you this to score points of pity. It's just to say where I've been, how things shook out. Now, the search for the father, the false idol, is over. Ruby is well enough. I have returned to the desert. And to the good hard work of writing and defending wilderness. Now I am here, it feels strange and good to know I'm not needing you, or any other man, in any particular way.

This is why I can tell you about a New Year's Day, not long ago, in our beloved Arches—when the sky is a gray roof, sheets of cold, galvanized steel. A day like this always chills down to marrow. But on this day in particular, I shiver violently—as I have for nineteen years. The day on which my father took his own life. He never got to meet #2 or #3. And he never got to meet Ruby, his grand-daughter.

I've been single for a good long while, not even a one-night catch-and-release. And now, after months and months of solitude—of bumping around in a foreign land in which no sign flashes familiar—there is another man, another speaker of this common canyon tongue, and I am here with him, stumbling down a blood red gully on which the faintest layer of snowflakes looks like lace. Or perhaps it looks like gauze—dressing for yet another wound.

Red flags would fly, I was sure of it. But there have been years of friendship in which everything has been unearthed, fingered, and held up to the sharp light of day. And now this new man and I have traveled to a new place in the park, a place I do not yet know, and this surprises. Because I have been here so many times—and I'll digress, to tell you about one trip, the time I brought my sister. It was my senior year of high school and I had learned enough from male mentors to know I could camp and explore without them. Now it was my turn to hand down what I'd learned. So I borrowed our dad's Blazer, the old metal Coleman cooler, and the very stove I've brought here to your grave. I drove us to Arches, set up camp, and said, let's go hike.

Suddenly, mid-tale, I'm not sure I want to keep

going. Because this isn't another story about my dead father. And it isn't a serial love story—the part I digressed from, the part about this new guy. And the part about my sister—it's not like I was hoping for some kind of Thelma and Louise thing, where we take back the redrock without a man. In fact, after all the effort, she returned to the car. So I delivered dinner to the front passenger seat. Put down the back seats and made her a bed. Then I threw my sleeping bag down in the luscious pink sand. In the middle of the night, a soft female rain turned torrential. Sheepishly I climbed into the back of the vehicle to sleep near my sister, who smoldered in my overbearing company. We drove home the next morning, in silence. We never saw Delicate Arch. We never even stopped at a pullout to take in the scenery—the grand and life-changing view.

Well, now. Come to think of it, these stories— when you include others in them, it complicates the narrative, doesn't it? I'm beginning to get why you wrote about solitude. Why the characters in your books were casual acquaintances, not intimates.

And still, I don't know that I can tell the story— about my time in Arches, or anywhere else—that simply.

TUKUHNIKIVATS,
THE ISLAND IN THE DESERT

That horse of mine, he raged when he could no longer ride out into the desert. The paddock had grown too small for him, and he once again bullied the other horses. So I loaded him in the trailer and drove him back to where he had come from—turning him loose at the base of the La Sals, where a herd of rescued equines was pastured. The lead mare and Dante hit it off instantly. As I walked away, he didn't look back; he was already in love again.

That's the story I tell myself, anyway. The women who ran the sanctuary said he came back angry, and so maybe he didn't look back because I gave up on him. Or maybe he knew I was giving up on other things that had allowed me the privilege of owning what is no doubt the most expensive of all pets—not that a horse is ever just that. A few months later, marriage #3 would end after seventeen years, and with it, everything I believed to be true about fidelity and intimacy and endurance. More than ever, these things seemed illusory. In the undoing, Dante likely felt abandoned again.

It would be two years before I could bear to visit that horse, but when I did, he came running—nearly crashing through the fence. The rest of the herd came too, but he wouldn't let them near me, not even his girlfriend. I wept openly, and he pressed his rosebud pink nostrils to my cheeks, as if he could wet-vac them off my face.

From my now-home just over the border, on a mesa in southwest Colorado, I can see the La Sals every evening and know what lives and gallops and bellows in their shadows. Only such a landscape could contain such a horse. Only the sky above it can hold such love and loss.

And now there's an aversion coming on, a flinching away from the loneliness I've worked so hard to cultivate. It once felt like the deepest expression of my wild nature, the key to real liberation, but now I'm not so sure.

EPISODES AND VISIONS

I'm kind of reeling here, Mr. Abbey. I got so carried away with what is beginning to feel more like a striptease than storytelling, that I kept at the whiskey and forgot to compensate with water. The sun has peeled off to the west, and no doubt the ice in your cooler has melted. I haven't once thought about food—save the cheese and apples, but those were hours ago. The mental bandwidth has mostly been dedicated to the desert. And to devotion. How the latter—both yours and mine—converges. And where it forks into separate channels.

So many journeys into Arches that I haven't yet told you about! Aside from that one with my sister, they were all made with men: My father, of course, many times. And then there was the one with a punk-rocker haircut—shaved on the sides and spiked down the middle—who couldn't appreciate the formations without first doing drugs. There was one who is now parked in a wheelchair and who never wanted to venture far from camp

even when he was ambulatory. And then there was
the one who insisted on cycling on the park's pave-
ment at a certain, intensified heart rate; I only saw
the shiny, padded backside of him as he pedaled
away for the day. Another dared bring his new
squeeze along for a day hike, and later he'd bruise
my arm for getting upset about it.

With each of these lovers, there was such in-
congruence: I just wanted to wander off the road,
off the trails, and get lost so I could feel my heart
beat as the blue note that it is—that precise, slightly
off-key sound that I had come to believe, after so
many warnings, so many failures, was like no one
else's.

But back to the New Year's Day in recent history. After so much solitude—which I felt even
when, *especially* when, I was part of a couple—there
is this man who has played for me his own blue
notes. And this time is the only time that things
have been pristine—there's not a single red flag
flapping in the wind that foretells of destruction.

Sure, I've worried that this will be yet another
year in which I'll somehow convince myself, as
in every other year, every other relationship, that
whatever I see in him must be a mirage—a projection of my own thirst. I worry that this will
be as bad as selling off land to oil companies,
and offering up land to recreationists who think
they are in love with the idea of wilderness, of

preservation, but really have the worst carbon footprint of all. I worry there will be toxic waste. I worry that the prehistory—the way I was before these casualties—will be erased, and I'll never reclaim the whole human I once was.

This is the grand illusion. That we were once whole. That our ecosystems were intact, self-sustaining. That everything we need is within—and to need others is as vampiric as drilling for every last drop of oil.

If this is why we seek solitude, we are in danger of extinction.

TERRA INCOGNITA:
INTO THE MAZE

Arches National Park, New Year's Day, 2017. Trump is now POTUS, which means "President of the United States," and though that acronym wasn't used during your earthly tenure, it's very hard for me to call that man by anything more formal or revering.

In spite of the pending doom he and his administration have cast over public lands, high notes drift in, courtesy of coyotes. Cognac is poured from the same Stanley flask. And there is a panel of rock art like none other.

We are far, far off the park's tourist beat, staring at a story line in which one person is tethered to another, and together they are connected to animals and horned deities. The line is etched deeply, like a thread of great tensile strength. This, I think, is what stitches the world together.

I stare and stare at the figures—beasts, gods, and humans. And everything in me—all that is primal, all that is spiritual, and all that is cerebral—comes together. In the gray flat light the dark patina warms oxymoronic: from cold red to hot cobalt.

I turn to the man beside me, and I see lines—story lines, bloodlines. But still no flags. I see him the way I see the redrock landscape around me, this park I've been coming to since I was a child. And the ways in which this man has been eroded means everything is exposed. He is the kind of topography I can follow. Through the dust devils and arroyo cuts and shifting sands. Through the damage, and the desire. This is what I know. This, too, is where I dwell. To touch his map is to put my finger on the rugged, broken terrain of my heart and say, right here, this is home.

And so this first day of the year blooms anew. I look around, at the red desert unfurling in every direction. I understand now, the way love is. The way we gather together what is beautiful, and what is broken. What is protected and what is predated. We love it with the whole of who we are. Even after, especially after, the carnage.

BEDROCK AND PARADOX

I mean no offense, Mr. Abbey. But here at the end of our time together I'll confess that *Desert Solitaire* didn't wow me to life-changing, yogic extremes. I chalk it up to being born here, in Utah. Every family endeavor—hunting, fishing, raising cattle, camping, skiing, and more—having happened on its public lands. Meaning much of what you noted in that book was something I had already noted for myself. I knew the species, the sensations, even before I had the words to name them.

But there came a day in high school when the boy I loved left me for, in his words, "some fresh action." My grades tumbled. I swapped the Go-Go's pop music for Suicidal Tendencies' punk. All because of a boy, I became everything I wasn't.

My English teacher, Mr. Krenkel, noticed and kept me after school one day. He was wearing a "Hayduke Lives" T-shirt because a local television station had visited earlier that afternoon to do a story on test scores or some stupid thing that you would surely have scoffed at. The principal had asked the male teachers to wear dress shirts and ties, the female teachers to wear skirts. He'd asked me too, as class president and occupant of other esteemed positions that reflected my compulsion to overachieve, to *please* take the safety pins out of my ears and leave the leather jacket and combat boots at home.

So I'm standing in Mr. Krenkel's class—he in his Hayduke shirt and me in my anarchy garb—and he hands me a map of the Escalante and a copy of *The Monkey Wrench Gang*. For spring break, he says, circling on the map the location of Hole-in-the-Rock Road, and the head of Coyote Gulch, go there. I say I've already been, with my dad. He says go again, but only after you read this book. I'll fail you if you don't.

I see now. Before that book, I'd taken the Utah wilds for granted. Assumed that it was safe because it was at the heart of God's gift to my ancestors. Besides, the best places were federally protected as parks and monuments and wilderness. Back then, I still believed such lands, their designations, were inviolate.

I went home and read about Doc Sarvis and Bonnie Abzug and Seldom Seen and Hayduke himself—and I was gobsmacked. I could *resist* authority! I could act on behalf of my heritage, by which I don't mean my Mormon ancestry but rather these beloved public lands! I packed up my Plymouth Champ and, with the punk-rock boyfriend who succeeded the first heartbreaker, drove south. We took LSD and headed into the canyons that now make up the Grand Staircase-Escalante National Monument, me with my dad's Kelty pack, the bottom of its external frame whacking the backs of my knees. I hardly noticed, because I fell in love in a whole new way. Not with the boyfriend, or the drug, but with the desert. Another wilderness activist was born.

And now, Mr. Abbey, that sun hangs like low fruit on the western horizon, and all around us the brown-skinned people to the south have begun to steal through the pooling shadows, where it's hard for the snipers to see them. As for me, I'm hungover and my thighs need a spatula to scrape them off this chair. I'm also wondering what the hell there is for dinner. I've brought my throwing knives, and I'm getting pretty good. Perhaps if I huck them out into the desert, I'll get lucky and hit a rabbit—a thought that I know makes you wince but right now I'm hungry enough to suck up my humane tendencies. Then again, if I throw into the dark I might puncture a water jug that could otherwise save someone's life.

Oh, the choices. And our complicity. Since your time in Arches, the art of survival, just like the search for solitude, has gotten far more complicated.

76

I'm all talked out. I had so many questions, so many narratives to pitch at your more dominant one—which I'm not faulting you for, by the way. After all, it was handed to you, that golden key to the ivory cabin.

Forgive me for saying this, but from where I sit, you're not quite the maverick you once seemed; I see your clones all the time and they are mostly heterosexual males with college degrees and devoid of much pigment. Even my friends, my fellow wilderness activist colleagues—men who say all the right things in the presence of women and the underrepresented others—they have made damn sure their places are retained at the head of the table, above the glass ceiling. Meaning I've been talked over, talked down to, hit on, and underpaid by those guys—and they are the closest thing I will ever have to brothers.

But I am not here to suggest we go our separate ways, we men and women. Lord knows I've had enough of that, and I'm betting you have too. In fact, there is nothing I want more than to go home to the blue-noted, flagless man, and I'm guessing you pine for your beloved in the same way.

Which leads me to the thing I've most wanted to say today: Would you mind me revising that phrase from the book—the one I lifted for my first wedding invitation?

What if it read: *Love flowers best in close quarters?*

It's not a question, actually. It's a must. We are on our way to being crammed together like cows in a feedlot. To survive without turning into heartless monsters, or soul-sucked automatons, we'll need intimacy with people every bit as much as with place.

The wound, the anger and apathy that masks it, is what drives us to be *le solitaire*—which in French refers to one who is isolated, a kind of "lone wolf." But the French form also means "tapeworm." Going it alone is a failure of contribution and compassion, and this is what drains the world dry.

Ultimately, this is why I am here today: to invite you to join me in asking your followers to do away with their rugged individualism—which I never bought anyway. By nature, we are a cabal. A group gathered around a panoramic vision. A group gathered to conspire, to resist. This is vital to our survival, as institutions fail and tyranny threatens. Believe me when I say that our democracy, with its wide but firm embrace of the last best wild places, has never been so jeopardized.

I actually prefer the French term, *cabale*. The *e* makes it a female noun, and that rings true about now. While *cabale* means political conspiracy and intrigue, it is imbued with spiritual and mystical meanings, too—and I'd say the divine thing we've been given is nature itself—both ours and the land's.

Our most precious resource now is wonder.

What we wonder about ignites our imagination, unleashes our empathy, fuels our ferocity. We fold in on ourselves, a thunderous, galloping gathering, a passionate, peopled storm, nearly indistinguishable from the ground on which it rains, on which it sprinkles seeds. This is how hope takes root. What springs forth are monolithic possibilities.

Despite all the bad news, the Monarch butterflies, once in desperate decline, have returned. For the first time in decades, a wolverine was spotted in Michigan. In defiance of Trump's predatory agenda, a coalition of 15 US states, 455 cities, 1,747 businesses, and 325 universities has proclaimed its commitment to the Paris Agreement, which seeks to rein in the horrific effects of climate change, on behalf of the American people. Today's millennials, a new generation of voters and consumers, have also unified and mobilized to shrink humanity's gargantuan carbon footprint. The snow leopards, four thousand in number and growing, have moved off the international endangered species list. Mexican fish are proved to be having cacophonous orgies, and California condors—of which only twenty-two individuals existed not long ago—now have numbers in the hundreds, some of them in southern Utah. Colonies of microbes have banded together in the ocean to devour swirling islands of human-generated trash. And get this: I saw two wolf pups and heard the howl of an adult—somewhere far from where wolves have been documented in the West. I won't say where, because it'll get them shot, but the wolves are spreading out, into the lands we love. Into Abbey's country. Amy's country. The people's country. Which was *Canis lupus* country all along.

Wait, before I leave, let me look in my pack. I'll have to dig through the rocks, snakeskins, and feathers collected on my way out to your final address—and yes, here it is: the original *Desert Solitaire* manuscript, with line-edits and corrections made by your own hand. It's a marvel, to hold these pages, typed by your fingers just a few years before I was born. Be patient, please, while I flip through this draft . . . there, I've found it . . . a very up-front reference to your wife and kids! Here, unlike a few other glossed-over mentions in the book—places where you dissemble and joke enough that we believe the nuclear unit to be hypothetical—it reads that you were a family man!

Why did you delete this line? Why is it that the juniper tree and the scorpion figure largely on the page when the people you loved do not?

This is so hard for me to understand. Because I write about the broken hearts. The infidelities. The suicides and separation of siblings. Perhaps this is the way of women: we seek not so much solitude as solidarity, intimacy more than privacy.

But it's the way of wilderness too—in a thriving ecosystem, integration matters far more than independence.

There is the adventure that traverses the land, that excites and restores. But there's also an inner landscape—its fiery furnace of the heart, the natural bridges built between beings. So I say to you, go solo, into the desert. Yes, do this and love every minute. But then come back. Come fall in with the *cabale* that has joined together, to save what we know and love. It will take multitudes to slow the avalanche of apathy. And it will take a lot of devotion.

The bats are bombing me now. And something large just passed by—whether it's a jaguar or a human heading north, I do not know. Really, they are one and the same, part of the world community to which we all belong—now, more than ever.

So thank you. For inviting us into Abbey's country. A lot of us grew and healed there. And we learned too what a privilege it is, to be stewards of these incomparable lands, to have the liberty to speak and act on their behalf. There, our hearts grew beyond the personal—with its small and selfish love affairs. But now our hearts must grow even beyond the political. Whether we're talking about the naked desert or the body, let us no longer duel in dualities.

Perhaps I can call you Ed, now that I'm packed

up and headed home. Kind of like the way we never speak to the folks we sit next to on planes and then suddenly we're all chummy as we prepare for landing—that rough, bumpy drop onto sweet bedrock holding the boundless whole of who we are: paradoxes, half-truths, and all.

AFTERWORD

Bears Ears Buttes, July 16, 2015. My grand-parents had prayed for the generations yet to come. That was me and many others beyond their sight. My role at this moment was that of an elected leader of the Ute Mountain Ute Tribe and co-chair of the Bears Ears Inter-Tribal Coalition, consisting of the Ute Indian Tribe of Utah, Ute Mountain Ute, Navajo, Hopi, and Zuni represen-tatives. Our vision and advocacy work unfolded as Standing Rock and Black Lives Matter were unfolding; women have stood, and still stand, at the center of these movements, too. The conver-sation on that day would forever change our lives and the future of Bears Ears, 1.9 million acres in the heart of the red rocks of southeastern Utah. These are the homelands and final resting places of my elders and ancestors and those of countless other indigenous peoples. The dances, songs, and prayers conducted since time immemorial lay out on this vast landscape of beauty. When I stood

out in the meadow at the base of the twin buttes
that rise like giant ears from the earth, I felt sad-
ness, unsettled grief, and self. So many places we
have known and depend on for both physical and
spiritual sustenance have been disrespected or
destroyed by others without the same connection
to the land. As the only woman member serving
on the Bears Ears Inter-Tribal Coalition, I had a
unique perspective and responsibility as we reached
across cultures to protect this sacred place. "I am
the land, the land is of me!" I heard that in the
gentle whispers from the wind blowing through
the pine needles. I remembered that the land is our
teacher, that everything radiates from the center.
A circle was created between two giant pine trees,
and members of the five Bears Ears Inter-Tribal
Coalition tribes, Department of the Interior rep-
resentatives, and Mother Earth gathered to share
what was in our hearts. I asked our Creator what
I could say that would convey understanding. The
answer was presented, and I responded: "Reach
down to the ground, clear away the pine needles
until you feel her. Touch our Mother Earth and
connect with her, allow her to tell you her story."
Hope, conversation, and my feet planted firmly
on Mother Earth, all served my commitment to
becoming her voice. If I could remain connected to
the earth, I could hear and tell her stories. Others
could and would listen.

~

The Utah Legislature's Commission for the Stewardship of Public Lands, April 20, 2016. I was asked to provide testimony to the Utah state legislators who serve on this committee as they considered a resolution opposing "unilateral use" of the Antiquities Act to designate national monuments in Utah. I flew in late the night before, adjusting my schedule to make the time to present to this distinguished group of Utah's elected leaders. I felt a great sense of honor to have the opportunity to conduct government-to-government business and develop relationships in my service to my tribal people. But I was not given the same respect by the chair of the commission, who cut me off and prevented me from delivering my prepared statement. I would have to say that this was a key moment in my deepening commitment to protecting and speaking for our Mother Earth. I would rely on the teachings of my grandparents and our Mother for strength to work even harder to protect Bears Ears.

Towaoc, Colorado, Fall 2017. I often reflect on the past to understand where it is that will need to be traveled. My grandparents used to tell us, "Know who you are and where you come from." I always thought my physical address and parents were all that I needed to know. It was a much deeper calling, and now I understand. My work as a tribal leader and co-chair of the Bears Ears Inter-Tribal Coalition has taken me on a journey with many roads, some faint at first, just as they appear when you do a fly-over of the region. But I had a clear starting point: my commitment to Bears Ears. Still, my journey continued to take me into sometimes unfamiliar territory, testifying at hearings, attending long meetings at the White House and Department of the Interior, and spending countless hours on my laptop as the Coalition prepared and then presented to the Obama Administration our proposal for national monument protection. My travels led me back home to my reservation, two hours away from Bears Ears, in Towaoc, Colorado. I always honor the words of my grandmother, the late Stella Eyetoo: "No matter where you go, always remember to come home."

Sleeping Ute Mountain, July 31, 2018. The smell of sage and blessing of rain out on the land. Brilliant red, orange, brown, and greens of many shades tell me I am home again—the colors you don't see when you are in the fast-paced lanes of metropolitan cities of our nation. I asked myself many times, how are we going to get the well-deserved protection, preservation, and continued access of this sacred area for the people? It appeared impossible! Then on December 28, 2016, President Obama

realized our vision and protected her, establishing
1.3 million acres as Bears Ears National Monument. Though it was smaller than the 1.9 million
acres we proposed, we were pleased that the monument proclamation included co-management
with Native leaders. This was such an important
moment for the five Native Nations of the Coalition, the twenty-six pueblos, and the countless
tribes and communities who supported us. Bears
Ears had been protected for our people, for all people and creatures, and for future generations. But
less than a year later, President Obama's successor
stripped away monument status from eighty-five
percent of the land and revoked tribal co-management, dismissing our work for protection and
healing. I went to the mountains and prayed. I sat
quietly and sang a song. I needed to soothe my
uncertainty and sense of being overwhelmed. As
I took in the air and felt Mother Earth beneath
me, I knew what it was I needed to do. First, have
faith in those prayers my grandparents laid out
on the land. Second, approach the continuing
conversations about Bears Ears with the thought
that I already have her protected. I can work from
within as though a national monument still exists
with the name of Bears Ears National Monument,
with a clear understanding that no matter where
the roads will lead us, I cannot enter into conversations defeated. Hope, faith, and grace were the

tools that my grandmothers bestowed upon me. As the only woman on the Coalition, I had to carry the strength and grace of my grandmothers. Grandmothers whose eyes have witnessed many generations of change to serve our people with hope, gratitude, and love. Resilience is the key, and we shall continue to be graceful, strong, and full of hope, remembering that the power of the world always works in a circle. The female voice is that of heart and family, of story and place. Today, I bring my story to these pages and a growing circle of leaders, families, hunters, writers, singers, and dancers connecting to our Mother. The sun will rise in the east and set in the west. Some things will never change, but what can be changed is self and purpose. I put my best foot forward to promote peace, love, and harmony for Mother Earth, my neighbors, and all people of this land, and join with others. Our voices rise in prayer, in song. Our stories, old and new, carry on the wind, through the pines, into streets and schools and churches, into voting booths and the halls of Congress.

Everything, now, comes full circle.

—Regina Lopez-Whiteskunk

Regina Lopez-Whiteskunk is a member of the Ute Mountain Ute Tribe and a contributor to the anthologies Red Rock Stories *and* Edge of Morning. *A former tribal councilwoman and co-chair of the Bears Ears Inter-Tribal Coalition, she serves as district director on the Montezuma-Cortez Board of Education in Towaoc, Colorado.*

ACKNOWLEDGEMENTS

Such gratitude to the cabal *and* cabale—all beloved sisters and brothers in arms who continue to resist the ravaging of Abbey's country and who believed me able to respond to *Desert Solitaire* in its fiftieth year:

Andy Nettell, proprietor of Moab's Back of Beyond Books and the man who first envisioned this essay, who then re-envisioned it as a work with a cover firm enough that it could stand on its own. This is not the first time he's pointed me to true north, and what a privilege it is, to have him in our ranks and as a friend. Kirsten Johanna Allen is not only an elegant editor and tireless advocate for Utah wilds, she made the vision of *Cabal* a reality. The *e* is for her. Mark Bailey, a shining star amid publishers and galaxies. Ken Sanders, of SLC's Ken Sanders Rare Books, brought insider intel along with boundless friendship—the man is all atrium and ventricle. Six extraordinary women, Shari Zollinger, Emily Shoff, Marcee Nettell, Kathleen Metcalf, Rachel Davis, and Anne Terashima provided indispensable feedback and deep smart polish. Amy O. Woodbury painted the red swell just as it feels—like saturation. The University of Arizona and Clarke Abbey provided the original, annotated manuscript of *Desert Solitaire*; all along, Clarke has also brought a generosity of spirit and dignity that thrums at the heart of this movement.

Redrock friendships are more durable than most. Holly Sloan and Colby Smith, a thousand lifetimes would not return the tethering and kindness—but I'll die trying. Sue Scavo and Bill St. Cyr taught me everything I know about the Underworld, and believed I could navigate the subtext in its depths. Craig Childs, no better brother, for wrestling mercilessly with me over title and truth. Daiva Chesonis, Lydia Peelle, Tim Lafferty, Blake Spalding, Jen Castle, Jim and Wendie Highsmith, and Regina Lopez-Whiteskunk . . . you were tailwinds while I talked to a dead man. Roy Vaughan, writing in the tree house, off the grid, made all the difference.

Thank you, Chris Weeks and Teague Eskelsen, for welcoming Dante back to Mt. Peale Animal Sanctuary & Healing Center. And for the forgiveness.

Charles Bowden taught me never to veer from the truth, despite stiff consequences. I'll be forever indebted to Jack Dykinga for making sure Chuck saw my first attempts to tell it.

My high school history teacher, John Mark

Krenkel, mapped the way out.

There is Ruby, in whom I see the preservation of the world.

There is Devin. At last. And always.

And there is Edward Abbey. Along with every knapped flake, whirled ammonite, and goshawk feather.

ABOUT THE AUTHOR

Amy Irvine is a sixth-generation Utahn and long-time public lands activist. Her second book, *Trespass: Living at the Edge of the Promised Land*, received the Orion Book Award, the Ellen Meloy Desert Writers Award, and the Colorado Book Award—while the *Los Angeles Times* wrote that it "might very well be *Desert Solitaire*'s literary heir." Her essays have appeared in *Orion*, *Pacific Standard*, *High Desert Journal*, *TriQuarterly*, *Climbing*, and elsewhere. Irvine contributed an essay to *Red Rock Testimony: Three Generations of Writers Speak on Behalf of Utah's Public Lands*, a book that was instrumental in President Obama's proclamation of the Bears Ears as Utah's newest national monument. She lives and writes off the grid in southwest Colorado, just spitting distance from her Utah homeland.

ABOUT TORREY HOUSE PRESS

Voices for the Land

The economy is a wholly owned subsidiary of the environment, not the other way around.

—Senator Gaylord Nelson, founder of Earth Day

Torrey House Press is an independent nonprofit publisher promoting environmental conservation through literature. We believe that culture is changed through conversation and that lively, contemporary literature is the cutting edge of social change. We strive to identify exceptional writers, nurture their work, and engage the widest possible audience; to publish diverse voices with transformative stories that illuminate important facets of our ever-changing planet; to develop literary resources for the conservation movement, educating and entertaining readers, inspiring action.

Visit www.torreyhouse.org for reading group discussion guides, author interviews, and more.

As a 501(c)(3) nonprofit publisher, our work is made possible by the generous donations of readers like you. Join the Torrey House Press family and give today at www.torreyhouse.org/give.

ABOUT BACK OF BEYOND BOOKS

Back of Beyond Books is an independent book-store in Moab, Utah, specializing in books of the Four Corners and the Colorado Plateau, including natural history, environmental literature, Native American culture, and western Americana, plus maps and guidebooks. We also feature a curated selection of rare and collectible books, maps, prints, and ephemera.

The genesis of the store grew from a conversation at Edward Abbey's memorial in May 1989, and Back of Beyond Books opened its doors in February 1990. The store's name was drawn from Abbey's novel *The Monkey Wrench Gang*. One of the gang, Seldom Seen Smith, was an outfitter, and the name of his company—and hideout—was "Back of Beyond."

Visit the store at 83 N. Main Street in Moab and at www.backofbeyondbooks.com.